MODA MALEFICARVM

- or -

The Dark Allure of Fashion

Otto von Busch

I say, wonderful are the hellish experiences,
Orphic, delicate
Dionysus of the Underworld.

D.H. Lawrence

Illustrations and collages by the author
with woodcuts from the *Compendium Maleficarum*

New York: SelfPassage
Ⓒ copyleft by the author 2016/2019
ISBN: 978-91-980388-5-9
[edit 1.2, November 2019]

Like your ghost in the mirror,
it always asks. Look at me.
Why are you ashamed to look at me?

There is a spectre haunting fashion, the spectre of witchcraft, a style incantation and conjuring of attention through the power of the will. Fashion is conscious manipulation of the embodied energies of glamour as a dark allure of social sorcery, of charms, cunning and carnal magic. Fashion, like witchcraft, is at heart a practice of shapeshifting and erotic shamanism.

As metaphysical alchemy, fashion designers engage in a continuously play with obscure references and symbols connoting social transgression, taboo and the mystic as well as malevolent sides of the human. Symbolic play in fashion appear as sigils, summoning demons of defiance and devotion, taboo and domination. They also call upon the insignia of the dark allure in sadism, masochism, and the intoxicating experience of defiling that which is considered pure.

Fashion ties into the energetic sources at the dark depths of experience. Through the embrace of taboo, it breaks through social barriers and connects erotic shadow works. Dissolving shame into pleasure, fashion intensifies the ambitions of the will. Shaping the body far beyond the light of reason, fashion emerges from the darkness of the world, through spiritual occultures and esoterrorism, and it slithers as a creeping underbelly of social relations. Savor such delicious sinfulness. Fashion as a wet dream; a tantalizing streak of erotic attraction and suppuration of fathomless desire, darkly blessed sexual mysticism in the lived realm of dressed, and undressed, craving. This is fashion beyond the symbolic, as an amoral engorgement of the enticing and luscious juices of flesh.

At its foundation, fashion is magic. Delicious, affirmatively untamed. The taste of honey, butter, and the warm arousal of bodies. It is an underwordly banquet of Dionysus.

~

Like witchcraft, fashion is often reduced to the manipulation of symbolic worlds, primarily concerning signs and language. But this is only one of its appearances. Instead, both witchcraft and fashion must be understood as sharing a liminal sphere of esoteric materialism. Surely, from a historical perspective, fashion, witchcraft and heresy have been used for symbolic rebellion, individual empowerment and usurping social hierarchies, bypassing political interests of clergy and nobility. But the importance of witchcraft, like shapeshifting, must be seen as a manipulation of material, esoteric and embodied matter, binding the imaginal spheres to the physical, biological to the social.

Fashion, as one of today's most powerful and encompassing aesthetic, esoteric and biosemiotic strategies of witchcraft and shapeshifting, is an explicit demonstration of a demonic reality. It exposes the most sublime unity between the esoteric and animalistic. The sorceress conjures a feral current. A force of possession, deliciously vile. An intoxicating hunger. Aesthetic ecstasy, the eschewal of a harrowing rupture.

~

Fashion is a natural condition of interbeing, amplified through the conventions of societal stratification and economic incentives. It is a labor of sensibility and affect, and it connects to the deeper instincts of erotic attraction and sexual arousal. Fashion must always be a canal knowledge and erotic liberation of a transgressive will.

Fashion is a conjuring of attention and attraction, the shadowplay of entwined wills. This makes fashion *a labor of allure*: it concerns simultaneously attraction and cunning, seduction and deception. It lures as much as entices,

pushes, coerces. The knowledge of fashion is not abstract; it is a highly sensorial capacity involving the whole physical body. And its reward and punishment is not only working in a level of intellectual awareness.

When fashion works at its best you *feel it*: the arousal, lubrication, horniness, tension, emission. It is an energy building up from the depths of the body, intensified through the dynamics of attraction. When fashion works at its best, it thrives in the same animalistic sensorium as the arousing labor and gratification in sexual conquest. An ordeal of dark healing.

~

Fashion is a carnal and corporeal knowledge and a biosemiotic practice. Surely, fashion may have meaning. It may play in the symbolic realm. But it uses signification as a living process, interconnecting evolutionary mechanisms of natural and sexual selection with the realm of embodied psycho-biological semantics. It works on the carnal and erotic levels, more than language and logics. It works on the body.

In this way, being fashionable is an affective labor, specifically in the meaning that there is a material and biological basis of its signs and processes of sign interpretation. And these signs attract and deceive, seduce and harm. Fashion is the merger between *Eros* and *Thanatos* in a lust for life.

In fashion, there is no clear distinction between flesh and soul, sin and virtue, domination and rebellion, life and death. Fashion is not good or evil, it affects us materially, making it warm or cold, hard or soft, it attracts or repels. It is an alchemy of the soul, a sanctuary from which the dark energies from an inner abyss can start carrying our body. This process of fashion is the ultimate *nigromancy*, the black magic and necromancy, in the glamour labor of fashion.

The fashionista is no victim of fashion, no slave, but a subservient and laboring worshipper of sensual esoterrorism with a beast stalking in pleasant guise, a sickly appetite to please. The allure, moment pierced, the silent stream of dark webs. A shudder, veils ripped. The burning member at the gate of the abyss, such glorious beacon of hell.

~

The allure of fashion not only works as a positive enhancement of social standing on an individual level. Like dark shamanism, fashion is also used against others, to manipulate peers and fend off rivals.

Fashion, as a charm, can be used for attack. Like malefic witchcraft, fashion can be an instrument to undermine the prestige or health of the victim, such as vilification, shaming or psychosomatic injuring of self-esteem. In such way, fashion is a *maleficum*, a wicked charm or vicious curse of witchcraft, an instrument of individual as well as social sorcery, and shrewd acts in the realm of human knowledge.

~

Fashionistas are considered shallow and untrustworthy, dealing in illusion and ephemeral relations. Yet they hold everyone's attention hostage. Historically, the persecution of witchcraft has been a continuous struggle over control and extraction, making magic practices scientific, predictable and quantifiable. The same mechanisms are at work in the construction and control over fashion as a ready-to-wear commodity: the control over carnal energies.

We must turn to magic to understand the fuller capacities of fashion. Each garment or accessory, each sign of allure is an *experimentum*, an effective spell, which in a material and biological way manipulates the biosemiotic social realm and guides the shamanistic journeys through inner darkness of the shadows.

~

The maleficium of fashion stands beyond good or evil. Maleficium connotes a social transgression of "evildoing," rather than metaphysical evil or supernatural magic. In this sense, fashion always has a tint of maleficium, of aesthetic disobedience, martial betrayal, the eruption of

uncontrolled desires and celebration of erotic ambition. It transgresses evil in the dark rivalry between peers courting the same mate, through the sinister social game of seductive antagonism and domination.

This kind of witchcraft is thus not gender specific but shapeshifts beyond human forms and physical appearances. Witches, incubus, succubus or other daimons of pleasure, can be of any form that matches their carnal embodiments or preferences. Yet, the prize in the contest is no simple matter, as fashion also takes place in a territorial competition for the ultimate sensorial reward. The orgasmic biosemiotic unity, healing the rupture of the bisected whole, the spiritual as well as carnal amalgamation of erotic dream bodies by real as well as symbolic fornication. Maleficum is the web of dark desires, spun uniformly by seduction as well as savagery.

~

In the medieval accounts of witchcraft, a sorcerer or witch was called a *maleficus* (male) or *malefica* (female), an "evildoer." As an intermediary between the virtuous ideals of the Christian heaven and the dark realism of hell, the witch's body and affects manifested a theological as well as vulgar battlefield. In 1487, the time of the infamous tract *Malleus Maleficarum*, Hammer of Witches, a plethora of theories were debated on

the material aspects of heavenly bodies. The debate also affected perspectives on how the dark crafts intersected with esoteric manipulation of the natural and social realms, and the cunning interference within the liminal domain of light and darkness. This debate can still seen in some of the euphemisms to witch, such as trickster, charmer or spellbinder.

Thus the primary tool for the witch's capability of cunning was *praestigium*. A praestigium is an enchanted spell, a capture and manipulation of attention, of cheating or deception. Fashion is a practical form of carnal cunning, a charm, a stolen look, a merciless capture of the victim's love and soul. Praestigium is a word with two etymologic suppositions; *praestinguō* ("to obscure, extinguish") and *praestringō* ("to blind; to blindfold; to dazzle or confuse someone").

Fashion is surely a form of cunning, a use of charm to manipulate attention, erotic forces and carnal realities. Fashion is one of many forms of *praestigium*.

~

Praestigium is the phantasm of demonic allure and carnal knowledge, the force of transvection in which the fashionista rides upon the demons of the underworld with Diana, Herodias and Salome, dancing through the seven veils and darkly gilded gates of the netherworlds.

The carnal reality and pleasures of demonic preastigium is proved by the forensic undeniability of nocturnal emissions. Such concrete and aqueous traces break across the sensoria so easily distorted by illusions, such as sight, to prove the full carnal reality of esoteric fornication, beyond the ratiocination of doubt. Arousal is a biological proof of a charm's esoteric power.

Thus fashion moves through the realms of symbolism, illusion or myth, towards ecstasy: the soul "standing outside" (ex-stasis) the body. In the mirror we meet a more true self, a shapeshifting hungry beast, draped in autoerotic desires, devouring our deepest drives for love and affirmation. The fashionista experiences its preastigium as a fully embodied carnal knowledge: desire, conquest, submission, the triumph of somatic satisfaction.

The succubus of style strikes through your ludicrously frail defenses. You appear starved as the night, before the force of lightning. Passion glisters on your blossoming skin; your triumph is your perfect obliteration into servitude.

~

Fashion and magic share a foundation of esoteric sexual spirituality. Both emerge from the intersection between erotic lucid dreaming, imaginal manipulation and biological functionalism. They share the same sensual reality.

In medieval times, a central component of witchcraft theory was the idea of demonic love, the devious and alluring sexual fantasies of the carnal knowledge offered by a incubus or succubus. Such dark "paramour" (*Buhl*) or "demon lover" (*Buhlteufel*) was a central agent to manifest the bond between the esoteric or spiritual, on the one hand, and carnal or bodily realms, on the other. As such, this was no trivial matter, as it intersected with the theological domain with the existence of angels and devils, the verisimilitude of the Gospel, sacraments, the *corpus verum* of the Eucharist, and in the end, the question if Christianity was superior to paganism.

According to these medieval ideas, both good and evil could be verified by *corporeal interaction* and carnal sensibility. The enactment of dark alluring passions could prove the links between the human and material realm to both the heavenly splendor and the continuous animalistic threat of wicked sinfulness. Sexually explicit dreams could prove the material existence of angels as well as demons. Witchcraft theory, in all its misogynic force, was a corporeal arena where the controversies of scholasticism took torturous form with a taste for blood and defilement.

But also fashion is a play with realities, and often proved real through acts of desecration, domination and hunger for blood, not least popular in the image of the vain vampire. Fashion is also such sadist wantonness, the piteous climax of death, fanged lips opened amorously. Each season an abyss of consanguinity, a birth in ecstasy, and a grave. The dark is calling for you.

~

In analogy with the medieval witchcraft theorists, we can know nothing about fashion and its labor of allure if we dare not be informed by demonic copulation. We know nothing about the seduction of fashion if we refuse to be aroused by it. The full body sensorium is a much more faithful witness than the so easily deceived sense of sight.

The quest for understanding witchcraft is not primarily a matter of asking if such theories correspond with reality, but rather, how do practitioners *believe* and *live* in their realms of somatic and carnal knowledge. In correspondence, the practical use of fashion, in its fullest carnal form, is to *test* and *enact* carnal knowledge of desire and allure: to practice biosemiotic praestigium.

Like lifting a leash around your neck, releasing the noose, fashion has no morality. No reproaches, no recriminations. It is its own selfish purpose. Like Eros, seduction cannot feel guilt.

~

It must be clear by now; to dress is a form of conjuring. To dress fashionably is a demonolatry and intentional worship and subservience to the esoterrorist forces of fashion. The fashionista summons the daimons and offers his or her body to be seduced and possessed. The seductive and sexual relationships mediated by this realm of biosemiotic praestigium manifest the carnal link between the world of fantasy and the world of flesh, a bridge suspended by the chains of *Eros* and *Thanatos*.

Fashion is the sexual submission and servitude to demons as defined by ritualistic acts and erotic soteriology: the forming of a pact in exchange for supernatural pleasures. A body enticed to live deliciously. The carnal knowledge fashion offers the merger of pleasure and comprehension, excitement and transvection on the forces of conatus. Carnal pleasure is the most intense and intimate form of human knowledge and gratification and the intensities of such biosemiotic knowledge stretches from the gentlest affirmation to full tantric orgasm, or from the faintest and featherlike sadism to full-blooded torture.

The magic of fashion grows in the fullest spectrum of our bodily sensorium. It animates an obscure realm, draped and veiled in dark and esoteric fantasies. Fashion, like a small adventure, is not premeditated. You become its prey. You serve a rapacious will, singing of pleasure, tense as a string under Orpheus' fingers.

From a socioeconomic perspective, witchcraft was, and still is, a contested arena of stratifying and destratifying forces, defying or even inverting hierarchical and horizontal loyalties and aspirations. Maleficum is a force that bypasses, but also evinces, cultural cementation processes. At Black Mass or Sabbat, witches repudiated their baptism and accepted a new name from the Devil, giving their clothes, blood and children to him and begged to have their names inscribed in his book of death. The very act included all forms of defilement and breaking of taboo, such as vowing to sacrifice children in the Devil's honor. After demonic fornication, the witches were then branded and marked by the Devil after repudiating the church's sacraments, and through every act invert the orders of heavenly virtue.

The rejection of every hypocritical virtue symbolized by the church was another link cut loose against social hierarchies and patriarchy. Practitioners become gods themselves, reclaiming their rightful superhuman domain, reborn as daimons, esoteric and liberated creatures never cultured by fear. They become pure appetites and cravings, possessive, desirous. Mean and vindictive. Obsessive and audacious. To the slaves of order, their unfettered attitude to a delicious life is always terrifying.

~

In many of the medieval scriptures on witch-craft, the Devil's rewards and punishments were not superhuman in the way presented in the myths of old Greece, where gods changed peoples' nature, gave powerful heavenly gifts, or annihilated them. Instead, like the local feu-dal lord, the Devil is very human or tyrant-like in his nature, behaving like a fully carnal hu-man. Similarly, the Sabbat is more like a darkly sybarite court than a purely spiritual domain, an arcane and hedonist carousal of unfettered sensibility with no spiritual promise except that of libidinous rapture. Indeed, only in exuber-ant sexual and animalistic embodiment can the spiritual manifest itself fully to the lascivious sensorial domain. Carnivorous and demon-like, and without guilt. Like a kiss of fire, it can have no guilt.

~

The maleficium of witchcraft is not wizardry, but the craft of twisting worldly powers in-herent in the spiritual realm to one's will. The witch is not the source powering the charm. Instead, the witch summons an alliance of eso-teric capacities, and is servile under the force of the demons, but also seduces them to bide to his or her wishes. Thus the witch *commissions* maleficia through an enactment of the pact with demons. The witch is thus not a sorcerer, as the dark shamanism is only channelled through his or her body and practices. The witch, like the fashionista, exploits the power of his or her medium to entice bodies to do their bidding.

Like fashion, the demonic reality is an elemental veil dividing the realms of flesh and soul, but it is also tailored and draped around bodies, and by its praestigium evokes fantasies while also incarnating and sensually sculpturing them to fit its servants. The dark temptation is a tainted impression of jet-black scintillance. Starless shadows rush in flickering patterns over a deep runnel. You dress, as to cup your hands to catch the dark stream. You end up empty-handed, sleeves soaked, drenched in perverse pleasure.

~

Fashion is allure set to work, a love under will. When working on our erotic dreamscapes, in shaping arousal, tension and release, it is a form of imaginal and carnal magic, sado-shamanism, a sensorial as well as sexual labor. The fashionista and witch shapes a practice, working at the boundaries of convention, social hierarchies, capitalism and power. On the one hand a master, on the other a servant. A succulent animation, intensification through transaction.

Like witchcraft, fashion practice is a pornophysical manipulation; a metaphysical and phantasmagorical, but also biosemiotic labor of prostitution to esoteric forces, a carnal servitude to fashion. The imaginal is an insatiable master hungry to be seduced, and rewards will be generously given to devoted worshipers.

In conjuring of aesthetic and sensorial stimuli repressed by social conventions the fashionista can shape-shift and break through the barriers separating *Eros* and *Thanatos*, life and afterlife, the carnal from the divine. Like fashion, this is to know demonic reality by experience, of voluntary subservience to carnal fantasies. The fashionista and witch are thus pornophysical expert witnesses to aesthetic and biosemiotic envy as well as pleasure, defilement as well as desire, and the full labor of allure.

~

As with the study of texts, we cannot fully know the intention of the witch or author of maleficia. Neither can we fully grasp the stimulant realm of the pornophysical if we only look at interpretation and the search for subjective or cultural meaning. Instead, maleficium, as a biosemiotic and neurophysical manipulation, must be understood as having a specific *intentio operis* (intention of the act itself). Maleficium operates on the body with an *economy of allure*, and invokes a principle of sensorial investigation that puts the act at the rational intersection between instincts defined by and drawn towards *Eros* and *Thanatos*.

There is no aim to maleficium or fashion other than carnal knowledge, its means and ends are intersecting esoteric as well as somatic pleasure. This is the spiritual reality craved by both angels and demons, but which is denied them both.

Savor it; the witchcraft of fashion, darkly, possessive. Taciturn consolations for demons. You are draped in the somber veils of morbid lust. Temptation, blindly delicate.

~

The spiritual fantasies merging with carnal knowledge in fashion is on a level of *virisimilitude*, or intensities of pornophysical realism and verisimilitude. An ecstasy of incubus and succubus; every new collection a black sabbat. Exaggerations and sexual hyperbole plays with textures, sizes and silhouettes of demonic sex fiends, mixing the proportions of the real with that of aggrandized and lubricated fever of salacious black vapor.

The maleficium of fashion is a promiscuous force, penetrating the victim like a *punctum*, a sensation of tearing a wound through the veils of carnal temptation. The Devil, as portrayed in many medieval images, reveals himself to the world as an androgynous creature with an abundance of enticing members and orifices: all portals to the painful carnal pleasures of demonic prurience. Savagery, glisten as silver, bodies rocking, the ecstatic caress in a bouquet of blood. A slow tyranny as the wounds secrete.

~

Most societies inculcate in their members the aversion to eat the flesh of their fellow beings. Like the beast and demon, the witch is an outlaw, and exists outside the conventions of society, rejected by the heavenly kingdom to stalk its outskirts. Yet the demon, as well as the witch, remains emperor-like and sovereign, in full command of its body, and without guilt or shame, an absolute Dictator or Dictatrix, a lord over the lower peoples of fear and convention. As an image, it may haunt conventional man, yet with its full demonic and carnal presence, it tears hierarchies apart by its unfettered passions, yet, viciously, with political demonology, reinstates them anew.

The witch, the demon, the fashionista; all are concepts with their nucleus at corporal interaction with erotic and daimonic reality, and all draw the carnal knowledge of maleficium into their orbits of delicious obscenity. In mutual blood, beauty pursed with sceptered terror, its treasure spilled, petals up, singing in carnal ecstasy. Its body stings like the vibrations of a bell. The bottom of its pit is cruel.

~

The balms and nectar streaming through me,
at the dead of night, in every drop of blood.
Look at me. Feast on my luscious darkness,
drink the juices of my daimoic flesh.
A beast, in my fashion.

Coda

To grasp the embodied experience of fashion we should approach it beyond a perspective of interpretation and meaning. To use Brian Massumi's phrasing in the foreword to Deleuze and Guattari's *A Thousand Plateaus* (1987) "The question is not: Is it true? But: does it work?" The question through which this narrative approaches fashion is in materialist or realist terms: how does fashion *work*, or more precisely, how does fashion *do its work*, how does it work on the carnal level, and *in the interest of whom?*

Fashion works *for* us, *with* us and *on* us. As a material as much as esoteric force, we get fashion to work for us, as we instrumentally employ it to engage in identification work as a material as well as immaterial labor: a *labor of allure*. As we ally with it, and dress fashionably, we align our desires and aspirations with our appearance, binding our aspirations to the second skin as a divination but also division of labor. As the garment makes my appearance alluring, it attaches some of its attraction to both my flesh and my soul.

But fashion also conditions and uses us as its vectors for other interests, like the selfish gene and extended phenotype acts in aesthetic selection, as pointed to in Nancy Ectoff's *Survival of the Prettiest* (1999). From the eyes of a fashionable garment, we are redundant organic bodies. The garment lives its fullest life glistening in the attention of others, not in the dark wardrobe: it needs to animate bodies in order to live. From such perspective, fashion is a living aesthetic phenomenon, an esoteric superorganism embodied in material culture. It moves over the seasons and ages, riding on our human desire for adoration and attention, freedom and distinction, progressing with us like a *perpetuum mobile*, as Zygmunt Bauman argues in his essay with the same title (2010).

Yet fashion is not only pretty: it is also grim. Like Fate, fashion caresses the few, but molests the many. Fashion is a cruel partner. It cares nothing about our frail bodies and wounded spirits. As we employ it in our social games, and form a pact with this social force, we are duped to run its interests. Its nature is daimonic. We use the affect of fashion in our carnal games, to lure and deceive, ensnare and reject. We seduce our prey and savage our rivals, with the help of fashion we transform our reality according to our will.

Fashion is used as an instrument to enhance our attractiveness in the processes of sexual selection, but we also employ it as a territorial marker and weapon in the process of natural selection, for predatory conquest against peers, rivals and prey. Fashion works as both a surface of beautification as well as bullying. From a realist perspective, fashion is part of Machiavellian games of merciless aesthetic rivalry, employing allure and deceit to produce adoration, one of the most powerful tools of domination known to man, making obedience and enslavement an experience of pleasure. We shape the world of attention, thriving in the insatiable desires for affirmation.

The labor of allure enacts itself on two different fronts or levels, with its subjects pinched between its double talons. One talon works on a level of human experience, where we struggle and compete utilizing fashion as an intersubjective weapon, using it in aesthetic rivalry to attract mates as well as fend off rivals. The other talon, pinching from the opposite direction, works on a more abstract level, but real nonetheless. It uses individuals as vectors for its own interests, preying on human vanity, pride and rage. Where I may use a prestigious brand to promote my chances of selection, I may sign a pact with forces beyond my control. In the end, in my success in the selection process, I have also worked for the brand, the meme, or cultural sedimentation mechanisms that I commissioned in my individual task. In the act of consumption, I choose servitude to the carnal elation offered by brands. I buy a charm of attention, and in exchange I offer my body, my pleasure, my attention, on the market of erotic mass-psychology.

This second talon enacts the force of fashion, possesses me, turning me into a passionate vector for its power. This is the same force of rage that Simone Weil captures in her essay *The Iliad, or the Poem of Force*,

> "The true hero, the true subject, the center of the Iliad is force. Force employed by man, force that enslaves man, force before which man's flesh shrinks away. In this work, at all times, the human spirit is shown as modified by its relations with force, as swept away, blinded, by the very force it imagined it could handle, as deformed by the weight of the force it submits to."

And as Peter Sloterdijk posits in *Rage and Time* (2010), the force in the *Iliad* is the rage that propels heroism. Achilles, possessed by rage, is the expression of strength, accomplishment, glory, vanity, ambition and the hunt for recognition. It is the hunger for glory that propels humans to strive for the higher deeds which later echo through the ages: accomplishments which blaze from the impulsive center of the proud self. The drive for attention is insatiable, the will to fashion ravenous. This is the pact man signs with gods or demons, which in turn are representations of our desirous and possessive appetites and cravings. In every new acquisition we sign a pact with fashion; this is the *passion for fashion*.

The labor of allure in fashion is an affective labor, it produces and modulates emotional and bodily experiences. As with fashion, we do not fully know what a body can do, or what unknown pleasures carnal knowledge can produce. On the level of affect, fashion uses the stimuli of the body to lure and entice, attract and capture, reject and destroy its prey. As affect, as a passion, it seeks not to convince us, it instead bypasses reason, mobilizing our neurobiology and incite us into action. As human organisms, we are biologically programmed to crave for pleasure and escape pain, and the processes *living* signification uses communication for coupling or rejection between living beings.

As biologists Humberto Maturana and Francisco Varela describe in *The Tree of Knowledge* (1987), all living systems are cognitive systems, and living is a process of cognition. The senses, which *brings fourth* the world to us, does not do so by communicating an abstract meaning as there is no "transmitted information" in communication. Communication takes place

each time there is behavioral coordination between organisms in a realm of structural coupling. Passion is the *real* labor in fashion; a crea-
tion and animation of fully carnal yet imaginal
worlds.

To understand fashion, we should thus not seek
the transmission of meaning, but the attraction
or rejection of coordinating behaviors and how
bodies interoperate through living sensorial ac-
tions and how bodies are affected on a carnal
level; through desire, arousal, and bodily emissions. To fully understand its magical powers,
we need to seek fashion in the carnal sensorium.

One could draw parallels to Paul Feyer-
abend's description in *The Conquest of Abundance*
(1992), how up until the renaissance the most
trusted human sense in the Christian world was
taste, and it was through the Eucharist, devouring the flesh and blood of Christ, that one could
get the most immediate relation to religious reality. Before the imaginative merger of math-
ematics, geometry and drawing with the inven-
tion of the perspective, the visual sense was not
trusted as providing much realistic proof of the
world. Instead, it was seen as easily deceived
and used for mockery and illusions. Thus a
truthful conception of the world was mobilized
through the other sensoria, and the more sensorial impact the higher degree of truthfulness.
In a similar way, we know the passions of each
other as we taste each other's desiring bodies.

Thus sight, and the quest for meaning, may reveal little about the workings of fashion. Instead, the carnal sensorium may give us a more truthful comprehension of what fashion *does with us*. Such perspective could be drawn from biosemiotics, such as in Jakob von Uexküll's (2010) *A Foray into the Worlds of Animals and Humans* and the many writings of Kalevi Kull on living semiosis.

The discussions above, on witchcraft and witchcraft theory, are heavily inspired by Stuart Clark's *Thinking with demons* (1997) and Walter Stephens' *Demon Lovers* (2002). However, in my search for a realist and carnal perspective on fashion, I have integrated Clark and Stephen's historic-theological expositions with a materialist and biosemiotic reading where the carnal interaction with demons is a form of supernatural coupling, the most complete merger of erotic and esoteric imaginal reality with the corporeal experience of orgiastic pleasure.

In a similar vein, while not subscribing to biosemiotics, Umberto Eco's arguments in *Interpretation and Overinterpretation* (1992) are useful to seek the enactment of symbols as a form of conjuring or organic couplings. Communication unites bodies, where the material intention of conatus pushes us to use fashion as *intentio operis* in the quest for coupling: either through love or through hate.

It is thus in resonance with biosemiotics we may get the fullest understanding of the labor of allure, that is what fashion *does*, as the sensorial pleasures are the most intense and intimate form of human coupling and knowledge. In accordance with the earlier discussion on sexual and natural selection, the intensities of gratification of such biosemiotic knowledge could be drawn along two forking trajectories. One line, the line of *Eros*, stretches a route of organic coupling, from the gentlest seductive affirmation to full tantric orgasm. The other, the line of *Thanatos*, draws a darker path of rivalry, defilement and destruction, from the faintest and featherlike sadism to full-blooded torture and domination. Yet the two are often intertwined and blend into each other, as erotic and sexual pleasures often override the misty veils between these seemingly opposite realms. We is well known to practitioners of sexual magic, exhilarating carnal knowledge arises from the defilement of the pure, attraction from pain, and fashion is seldom shying away from such mechanisms, restraining or piercing the flesh in order to propel the delicious intensities of pleasure.

The labor of allure must thus be understood as a materialist conjuring, and that is why witchcraft is such fertile ground for understanding fashion as both embodied and imaginal practice. Witchcraft, cunning and maleficium help reveal the instrumental use of sensorial manipulation in human coupling. As mentioned before, the spell, or *praestigium* is a form of cheating or deception, a practical form of cunning, a glamorous spell, a "charm." And like glamour, charm is attraction, but it is also, as suggested by the two etymologic suppositions of *praestigium*, "to obscure" as well as "to blind; to dazzle or confuse."

Building on Elizabeth Wissinger's concept of "glamour labor" in *This Year's Model* (2015), the labor of allure is working with the refinement and cultivations of affect. However, as mentioned above, the labor of allure stresses the materialist merger of the two selective principles, of sexuality and rivalry, *Eros* and *Thanatos*, as the cultural and evolutionary force of fashion. The labor of allure is a *realist* labor in fashion, it is enacted in a world of winners and losers, power and servitude.

In order to understand fashion, as medieval theologists were trying to understand witchcraft, we need to grasp the carnal knowledge arising from the forking trajectories of the two selective principles. We need to acknowledge carnal experience as the motor of fashion and that a labor of allure enacts both these forces, of seduction and domination, pain and pleasure, to see how fashion merges the realm of fantasies with the realm of flesh. Through the labor of allure, fashion acts as a mechanism of biological coupling through carnal knowledge, driving us towards seduction or rejection, transvecting the force of conatus.

Yet, each of us, being subservient to fashion through a pact, are in a drawn into a transaction of two interfolded processes of animation. The consumer buys a sense of erotic affirmation, while selling his or her body as a vector for realization. Fashion is always an erotic labor. It is the carnal pleasures that enact fashion, a pact with a daimonic reality in exchange for delicious pleasures. On a scale of superorganisms, this transaction is a form of prostitution to the real political interests of memes, markets or selfish genes: pinched between the double talons of fashion. This makes our labor of allure always take place as a matter of servitude; we purchase fashion and we are simultaneously bought to run its interests. We become fashion's phantasmorgical yet real prostitutes: its πόρνη (pórnē).

The labor of allure is the *pornorealism* of fashion, a carnally explicit will to live deliciously. I say, wonderful are the hellish experiences of such pleasures.

9 789198 038859